EMPLOYEE DISMISSAL:
PRACTICAL SOLUTIONS FOR EMPLOYERS

EMPLOYEE DISMISSAL:
PRACTICAL SOLUTIONS FOR EMPLOYERS

LEE SU TENG & ONG LIN DAR

PARTRIDGE

Copyright © 2019 by Lee Su Teng & Ong Lin Dar.

ISBN:	Softcover	978-1-5437-4915-1
	eBook	978-1-5437-4916-8

All rights reserved. No part of this book may be used or reproduced by any means, graphic, electronic, or mechanical, including photocopying, recording, taping or by any information storage retrieval system without the written permission of the author except in the case of brief quotations embodied in critical articles and reviews.

Because of the dynamic nature of the Internet, any web addresses or links contained in this book may have changed since publication and may no longer be valid. The views expressed in this work are solely those of the author and do not necessarily reflect the views of the publisher, and the publisher hereby disclaims any responsibility for them.

Print information available on the last page.

To order additional copies of this book, contact
Toll Free 800 101 2657 (Singapore)
Toll Free 1 800 81 7340 (Malaysia)
orders.singapore@partridgepublishing.com

www.partridgepublishing.com/singapore

CONTENTS

Introduction ix

Chapter 1   Dismissal for Misconduct: Absence
            and Sleeping at Work 1
    Case 1 : Intan Sofia Binti Zainuddin v Toi
             Toi Services Sdn. Bhd 3
    Case 2 : Sandran a/l Perumal v Nestle
             Manufacturing (M) Sdn. Bhd. 4
    Case 3 : Aezrine Shah Bin Abdullah v Fat
             Boys Records Sdn Bhd. 5
    Case 4 : Seerangan A/L Kuppusamy v Maju
             Jutabina Sdn. Bhd. 6
    Case 5 : Thilaga Valli A/P Subramaniam v
             A Hartrodt (M) Sdn. Bhd. 7
    Employer's Tips 9

Chapter 2   Dismissal for Misconduct:
            Insubordination 11
    Case 1 : Ngiam Geok Mooi v. Pacific World
             Destination East Sdn. Bhd. 13
    Case 2 : Kong Seng Chai v Perusahaan
             Otomobil Nasional Sdn. Bhd. 14

Case 3 : Sin Kok Foong v Grey Worldwide
  Sdn Bhd. 16
Case 4 : Encik Roslan Bin Yussof v
  Toyochem Sdn. Bhd. 17
Case 5 : Suresh Kumar Muniandy v. Kilang
  Makanan Mamee Sdn. Bhd. 18
Employer's Tips 20

Chapter 3 Dismissal for Misconduct: Sexual
  Harassment 22
Case 1 : Mohd Ridzwan Abdul Razak v
  Asmah Hj Mohd Nor 24
Case 2 : Mohd Nasir Deraman v Sistem
  Televisyen Malaysia Berhad (TV3) 26
Case 3 : Khoo Ee Peng v Galaxy
  Automation Sdn. Bhd. 28
Case 4 : Encik Edwin Michael Jalleh v
  Freescale Semiconductor Malaysia
  Sdn Bhd 30
Case 5 : Ahmad Ibrahim bin Dato Seri
  Mohd Ghazali v. Augustland Hotel
  Sdn. Bhd. 31
Employer's Tips 32

Chapter 4 Termination of Probationers 35
Case 1 : Indra Devi a/p Rajoo v. Everhome
  Furniture Mfr (M) Sdn. Bhd. 38
Case 2 : Lee Pei Sze v. Swiftlet Garden Sdn. Bhd. 39
Case 3 : Tan Cheng Leng v Tropicana
  Medical Centre (M) Sdn Bhd 40
Case 4 : Hari Bala A/L R. Parasuraman v.
  Johnson Control (M) Sdn. Bhd. 42

Case 5 : Azizah Binti Ahmad v Malayan
              Banking Berhad.. 43
    Employer's Tips.. 44

Chapter 5   Poor Performance...................................... 46
    Case 1 : Raja Azmil Bin Raja Hussein v
              CIMB Bank Berhad 47
    Case 2 : Yong Mee King v Kasyaf Bina Sdn Bhd..... 48
    Case 3 : Raffan Kashoggi Bin Ramli v
              Nectar Agro (M) Sdn. Bhd. 50
    Case 4 : Hasdie Bin Tusin Against Kudat
              Golf v Marina Resort (Tangamahir
              Sdn Bhd) 52
    Case 5 : Norhayati Binti Sulaiman v Shell
              Malaysia Limited 54
    Employer's Tips and Recommendations................ 56

Chapter 6   Redundancy... 58
    Case 1 : Mariana Binti Hassan v British
              American Tobacco (Malaysia) Berhad..... 59
    Case 2 : Kuldip Singh A/L Sarban Singh v
              Ismeca Malaysia Sdn. Bhd. (IMAL)......... 61
    Case 3 : Suzielly Sheilly Bt. Z Mambang v
              LF Asia Sebor (Sabah) Holdings
              Sdn. Bhd. 64
    Case 4 : Syd Hashim Bin Syed Othman v
              Ismeca Malaysia Sdn. Bhd 65
    Case 5 : Vijayakumar A/L K. Bathumalai v
              Inter Data Technologies (Malaysia)
              Sdn. Bhd. 66
    Employer's Tips.. 67

Chapter 7 Retrenchment 68
- Case 1 : Maimunah Binti Daud & 8 Others v GG Timur Trading 69
- Case 2 : Maser Sdn. Bhd. v. Yeoh Oon Wah 70
- Case 3 : Vijayakumar A/L K. Bathumalai vs Inter Data Technologies (Malaysia) Sdn. Bhd. 72
- Case 4 : Vijayapal Singh A/L Hira Singh v Kelab Sukan Pulau Pinang 74
- Case 5 : Hotel Jaya Puri Bhd v National Union Of Hotel, Bar & Restaurant Workers & Anor 78
- Employers Tips 79

Chapter 8 Constructive Dismissal 81
- Case 1 : Kilang Beras Ban Eng Thye Sdn Bhd v Yacob Bin Noor Mohamed & Anor 82
- Case 2 : Forari Corp Sdn. Bhd. v. D Sharil Bin Harun 83
- Case 3 : Dr. Rayanold Pereira v. Menteri Sumber Manusia & Anor ([1997] 3 CLJ Supp 116) 84
- Case 4 : Kenneison Brothers Sdn Bhd v Selvaratnam 85
- Case 5 : Joo Sim Kee v Patent Licht Bulbs & Lamps Sdn Bhd 86
- Employer's Tips 88

Appendix 91
- Code of Conduct for Industrial Harmony 91

INTRODUCTION

The awareness about employee rights in Malaysia has increased over the years. Unfair dismissal can be brought to the Industrial Court. Employees are entitled to claim for reinstatement to the former employment or compensation in lieu of reinstatement and back wages when they have been wrongfully dismissed.

Section 20 of the Industrial Relation Act 1967 of Malaysia sets out a provision to challenge termination of employment. This section provides an employee (irrespective of income level) who claims that he or she has been unfairly dismissed to make a representation to the Director General for Industrial Relations ("Representation") within 60 days from the date of dismissal.

The appellant can make the representation to the Industrial Relations department either by writing to the Director General of Industrial Relations (DGIR) or personally file in the office within 60 days from the dismissal. A conciliation session will be arranged between the employer and the aggrieved party to reach an amicable settlement. The employee can be represented by the union or Malaysian Trades Union Congress (MTUC). While the employer can be represented by the Malaysian Employers Federation (MEF). DGIR will extend the case to the Minister of Human Resource (MOHR) if conciliation fails. MOHR will hold the discretion to determine if it is fit to be referred the unresolved case to the Industrial Court.

The Industrial Court will then assess if industrial harmony exists between the two parties and if reinstatement is appropriate. If the court held that no reinstatement is allowed, the employer will be ordered to pay back wages and compensation in lieu of reinstatement to the claimant. The decision made by the Industrial Court is final, however, it can be challenged in the High Court.

It is with this in mind, this book serves as a reference tool on the employment issues that you may have. Court awards, which are readily available online for public access via www.mp.gov.my/en/ have been summarised for your easy reference and the following are the actual employment cases and practical solutions for further illustration:

1
DISMISSAL FOR MISCONDUCT: ABSENCE AND SLEEPING AT WORK

It is a basic obligation of an employee to be present in his or her employer's workplace during the time at which he or she is required to be at work. Absence without prior approval, including coming to work late and sleep during working hours, constitutes to violation of discipline. A one-day absence or a single act of misconduct may not warrant serious disciplinary punishments. However, habitually absent without good reasons as well as excessive tardiness (failure to observe the company's working hours) amount to serious misconducts, which warrant dismissal from employment.

Section 15(2) of the Employment Act 1955 provides that:

"An employee shall be deemed to have broken his contract of service with the employer if he has been continuously

absent from work for more than two consecutive working days without prior leave from his employer, unless he has a reasonable excuse for such absence and has informed or attempted to inform his employer of such excuse prior to or at the earliest opportunity during such absence."

Regular and punctual attendance is important for the employer to ensure smooth running of the company. A survey by the Malaysian Employers Federation (MEF) found that Malaysian companies suffer more than RM6bil in yearly costs for lost man-days through the absence of their employees.

Employees can only go on leave if there is an express approval given by the employer in advance. Leave application must be applied in advance and in accordance with the company's procedures by all employees unless on emergency grounds. In the event of sickness, according to the Employment Act 1955, Section 60(F), an employee who absents himself or herself on medical leave is required to inform the employer of his or her illness within 48 hours of the commencement of the sick leave.

In unforeseen circumstances, the employee should give a good excuse for his or her absence. He or she ought to make reasonable efforts to inform the employer about the absence at the earliest time possible and obtain the oral approval. Failure to do so would be considered as an act of insubordination. Likewise, the employee needs to submit leave application after the emergency leave and provide any relevant documentary proof to the employer.

Grounds for Lawsuit against Employer

Case 1 : **Intan Sofia Binti Zainuddin v Toi Toi Services Sdn. Bhd**

Case No. : 3/4-106/15
Award No. : 1089 of 2016

Ms. Intan Sofia Binti Zainuddin, an Account and Admin Executive at Toi Toi Services Sdn. Bhd., was dismissed for sleeping during office hours during her pregnancy. The court found that her dismissal was without just cause or excuse.

Ms. Intan was found sleeping at her desk for two hours on 8 January 2014. The company issued a show cause letter to Ms. Intan on 15 January 2014 with regard to the incident. She explained verbally to her superiors about her condition. She admitted that she had fallen asleep at her desk as she was experiencing morning sickness and on medication. On the same day and within hours, the company gave a termination letter to her.

The court found that no warnings had been given to her prior to her dismissal. The court pointed out that Ms. Intan was not given a chance to defend herself and provide proof of her condition. Furthermore, she did not have any previous disciplinary record.

The court concluded that the punishment imposed on Ms. Intan was too severe. Being caught sleeping in the office merely once does not warrant a dismissal.

The Employer Wins

Case 2 : Sandran a/l Perumal v Nestle Manufacturing (M) Sdn. Bhd.

Case No. : 4/4-335/12
Award No. : 1792 of 2013

Mr. Sandran worked as a Technical Operator at Nestle Manufacturing (M) Sdn. Bhd. He was dismissed by the company on the allegation that he was absent from work from 25 to 27 October 2010 without obtaining prior approval.

His justification was that he had to rush back to Nilai to settle his family's land matters. After he returned work on 28 October 2010, he was issued a show cause letter to explain his absence from work. His superiors concluded that the reasons for his absence was unacceptable and the land matter was not an emergency matter. Mr. Sandran failed to prove that his presence at his hometown to solve the family's matter was urgent.

The company had already given him several opportunities to redeem himself and to change his behaviour of lateness and absenteeism, but when he was absent for three consecutive days without permission and failed to give proper explanation, there was no other option but to dismiss him.

The Industrial Court found that the dismissal was justified considering his past disciplinary record and long absence without excuse.

Case 3 : **Aezrine Shah Bin Abdullah v Fat Boys Records Sdn Bhd.**

Case No. : 19/4-934/14

Award No. : 443 of 2017

Mr. Aezrine Shah, an Art Director at Fat Boys Records Sdn. Bhd., lodged a complaint that he had been forced to resign. He claimed that he was threatened during a meeting with the company's CEO. He was accused with several allegations of misconduct, including the allegations that he came in late for work.

Mr. Aezrine was not given reasonable time to deliberate or seek advice on the resignation matter. He had no other choice but to sign the resignation letter during the meeting. The court held that he had indeed been dismissed in this manner.

However, the court found that he, himself, had contributed to his own dismissal by habitually coming in late. Mr. Aezrine admitted that his immediate superior had cautioned and scolded him on his excessive tardiness. Also, he did not deny that he came late to work as frequent as three times a week and the lateness varied from half an hour to three and half hours.

Case 4 : **Seerangan A/L Kuppusamy v Maju Jutabina Sdn. Bhd.**
Case No. : 12(24)(4)(24)/4-126/12
Award No. : 206 of 2017

Mr. Seerangan, a T-Rex Operator at Maju Jutabina Sdn. Bhd., was dismissed by his employer on the ground of unsatisfactory attendance records. He was found guilty of habitual late attendance. Although he had been warned several times, he continued to come late to work and had taken the matter lightly. Besides, his superior discovered that he was continually absent from his designated work station without permission. His presence at the work site was crucial to ensure the operation runs smoothly.

Mr. Seerangan also went on leave without approval. He assumed that he only needed to notify his supervisor about the leave and need not apply for it. He did not fill in the leave application form and proceeded to be absent for two days.

He even made disrespectful comments and false accusations on his superiors. He would set a bad example to the other employees if no actions were taken against him. Hence, the company had no other alternative but to dismiss him.

The court found that the excuses given by Mr. Seerangan were unacceptable and his attitude towards his superiors was intolerable. His dismissal was upheld.

Case 5 : **Thilaga Valli A/P Subramaniam v A Hartrodt (M) Sdn. Bhd.**

Case No. : 17(14)/4-1026/13

Award No. : 1321/2017

Ms. Thilaga Valli alleged that the termination of her service during her probation period was without just cause or excuse. She was appointed as Key Accounts Development Manager by A Hartrodt (M) Sdn. Bhd. She was accused of not complying with the company's guidelines on punctuality. She was expected to be punctual, but failed to do so on numerous occasions. Her daily attendance report clearly indicated that she was late for work for 9 out of 15 days.

Ms. Thilaga admitted she was persistently late for work, but she claimed that a few minutes late to work had no significant impact on the company. The court found that her act was unacceptable, particularly because she was still a probationer at the company. Regardless, whether she was late to work for a few minutes or longer, it is irrelevant and constitutes a misconduct.

Other than lateness, Ms. Thilaga was alleged to make adverse remarks against the company and her superior to other colleagues on several occasions. She did not deny the allegation, but claimed that she did it during lunch hour and after working hours. Besides, she also had an argument with her superior in the office of the Managing Director.

Her superior had force open her drawer to retrieve the company's laptop. Ms. Thilaga accused her superior had conducted a mock auction to auction her property. However, the court found her allegation was baseless and the action taken by the company was appropriate.

The court concluded that her habitual lateness and insubordination act against her superior proved that she was an irresponsible staff, and therefore she did not deserve the confirmation from the company.

Employer's Tips

1. Inform all employees that having proper attendance is crucial.
   - Formalise the company's expectations for attendance by having an attendance policy or include the expectations in the company's handbook.
   - Keep a proper attendance record to assist the company in handling any subsequent actions against the employees, including issuance of warning or show cause letters, domestic inquiry, etc.
   - For severe attendance issues, the company may encourage full attendance and punctuality by giving out incentives for punctuality or having no unplanned absenteeism; or include attendance as one of the criteria in the employees' KPI.

2. Leave application procedures.
   - Provide information and guidance for managers dealing with requests for leave including emergency leave.
   - Inform all employees about the procedures for leave application. All employees should apply for leave in advance and get prior approval from their superior(s).
   - All leave application must be documented. If the leave is not approved, the employee should be informed accompanied with reason of rejection.
   - Monitor the employees' use of emergency leave carefully and put in measures to avoid abuse.

3. Issue reminders and warning letters to habitual absentee.
    - Investigate the absence and act with due care in taking disciplinary action.
    - Provide advice and counselling to the employee who is always absent or come in late to work. Give the employee an opportunity to change his or her misbehaviour.
    - The counselling session should be recorded. A summary of the discussion should be acknowledged by the employee.
    - A warning letter should be issued if the same misconduct is repeated. Give a reasonable period of time to respond to a show cause letter.
    - Proceed to hold a domestic inquiry if the response by the employee is not acceptable.

4. Show more initiatives to promote mental health care and stress-free culture in the workplace.
    - Invest in employees' mental health and emotional well-being as positive workplace culture would lower incidences of absenteeism and frequent illness.

2

DISMISSAL FOR MISCONDUCT: INSUBORDINATION

An employee is required to execute his or her duties as expected of him or her under the terms and conditions of service. He or she must act faithfully and in accordance with the interest of the employer. In Ngeow Yoon Yuan v. Sungai Wang Plaza Sdn. Bhd./Landmark Holdings Bhd. [2006] 2 CLJ 837, the court pronounced that:

"In Malaysia, the general rule governing the doctrine of superior orders is nothing more than the duty of obedience that is expected of an employee. The most fundamental implied duty of an employee is to obey his employer's orders."

If an employee fails to comply with any lawful and reasonable orders given by his or her employer, he or she is guilty of insubordination. Examples are:
- Challenges the authority of the superior.

- Refusal to obey the superior's legitimate instructions and orders.
- Deliberately violate the company policies, procedures, rules and regulations.
- Public criticism of the superior or the company.
- Repeatedly display disrespectful and rude behaviour towards the superior. For instance, use insulting and abusive language towards superiors.

Companies will not be capable to operate effectively if their subordinates refuse to comply with each and every legitimate order from their immediate supervisors. The act of insubordination can be viewed as a serious misconduct as it breaks the trust and confidence between the employer and their employees.

What if the employee thinks the order given by his or her employer is wrong? The Federal Court stated:

"If the employee takes it upon himself to disobey the order which he thinks to be unlawful and unreasonable two courses are open to him. He can point out his difficulties, if any, to the superior and if the latter insists on the order being carried out, he can do the work and take the matter further in proceedings against his employer or to complain to his union. If he disobeys, he must take the risk if the court finds the order to be lawful and reasonable."

Insubordination cannot be tolerated by any employer in order to maintain discipline among employees. The act warranted the punishment of dismissal.

Grounds for Lawsuit against Employer

Case 1 : **Ngiam Geok Mooi v. Pacific World Destination East Sdn. Bhd.**

Case No. : 10(9)/4-875/12
Award No. : 608 of 2014

Ms. Ngiam Geok Mooi, a Regional General Manager, had been working in Pacific World Destination East Sdn. Bhd. for 20 years. She had an unblemished employment record. However, she was dismissed from employment for refusal to report to and obey the instructions by her superiors. She then sought for a remedy under section 20 after termination.

Ms. Ngiam claimed that she refused to make adjustments to the company's budget as she believed it was an unrealistic budget proposed by her two superiors. She also wrote an e-mail saying she would no longer report to her superior.

The court found that she was indeed guilty of insubordination, but the penalty to terminate her service was indeed too severe and disproportionate to the misconduct committed by Ms. Ngiam. She had committed a single act of misconduct. The dismissal was therefore without just cause or excuse. The court ordered the employer to pay compensation in lieu of reinstatement and 50% scaled-down back wages to her.

The Employer Wins

Case 2 : Kong Seng Chai v Perusahaan Otomobil Nasional Sdn. Bhd.

Case No. : 3(13)(25)/4-844/14
Award No. : 465 of 2017

Mr. Kong was appointed as the General Manager of Supply Chain Management at Perusahaan Otomobil Nasional on a 3-year contract basis. After 14 months in his service, he received a show cause letter from the company for three charges. The charges were, not wearing a necktie at the Task Force Customer Complaint Meeting, leaving the meeting room after a senior member of the management team asked him to wear a tie, and failing to make the scheduled presentation during that meeting.

Mr. Kong was aware that he had to deliver the presentation at the meeting. But he claimed that he thought his presence was not required as he had been waved out of the meeting by the company's sector head – Technical Operations. He then proceeded to work as usual in his office. The meeting recorded that he was 'MIA' (missing in action).

The court found that Mr. Kong was guilty for not wearing a tie during the meeting with the higher management. It was not in line with the company's rules and guidelines of the dress code. Although not wearing a tie can be considered as a minor misconduct, the court agreed that his failure to make the presentation to the company's senior management officers was a disobedient act. He was clearly insubordinate and guilty for the second and third charges.

The court confirmed the decision of the company in terminating Mr. Kong was appropriate and the dismissal was with just cause and excuse.

Case 3 : **Sin Kok Foong v Grey Worldwide Sdn Bhd.**

Case No. : 12/4-678/15

Award No. : 1460 of 2018

Mr. Sin Kok Foong was a Group Executive Creative Director in Grey Worldwide Sdn Bhd. There were six allegations against him in the show cause and dismissal letters. He denied all of them and tried to justify his act of insubordination against his immediate supervisor's, i.e. the CEO. He was dismissed by the company on the grounds of repeated acts of indiscipline and insubordinate behaviour. Although there was no domestic inquiry held by the company, the court found his dismissal was with just cause and excuse.

Mr. Sin was instructed to participate in a Performance Improvement Plan (PIP) with the CEO due to his poor performance and leadership skills. Nevertheless, he refused to sign the PIP, failed to comply with the terms listed in the PIP, and failed to submit the weekly report and meet with the CEO to discuss his progress on a weekly basis. Despite receiving the warning letters to comply, he refused to obey the CEO's instructions. The language he used in his emails and letters to the CEO were rude and insulting.

The court found the company would not be able to trust and have confidence in him as an employee due to the cumulative misconducts of insubordination. Thus, Mr. Sin's claim that he had been dismissed without just cause or excuse was unfounded.

Case 4 : Encik Roslan Bin Yussof v Toyochem Sdn. Bhd.

Case No. : 10/4 – 876/10
Award No. : 502 of 2012

Encik Roslan worked as an Assistant Production Supervisor at Toyochem Sdn. Bhd. He lodged a claim for reinstatement to his former position upon being dismissed by the company. He had been accused for persistently challenged the company's authority. The allegations towards him were refusal to follow the company's lawful instructions to sign the attendance book, submit daily reports, and prepare the assessment of claims. Encik Roslan claimed that the instructions were invalid as they came from the Human Resource Manager who was not his immediate superior.

During the domestic inquiry, the company found that Encik Roslan was guilty for using abusive language towards his superior. It happened when his superior tried to pass a letter from the Human Resource Department to him. The letter was about his frequent abuse of sick leave. He threw the letter to the ground and blamed his superior for the issuance of that letter.

Encik Roslan denied the company's allegations. However, the court found that the domestic inquiry was valid and concluded that misconduct of insubordination by him clearly warrant the extreme punishment of dismissal.

Case 5 : **Suresh Kumar Muniandy v. Kilang Makanan Mamee Sdn. Bhd.**

Case No. : 5/4-781/10
Award No. : 1154 of 2013

Mr. Suresh Kumar Muniandy was employed as a Production Supervisor at Kilang Makanan Mamee Sdn. Bhd on a 6-month probation period. The company decided to extend his probation period for another three months on the grounds of unsatisfactory work performance. The review of his performance was documented and accepted by him.

Although the company was willing to give him some time to improve, he refused to sign the extension of probation letter. During the discussion together with the Factory Manager and his immediate superior, he insisted not to sign the letter but he still wants the job. As a result, he was terminated due to his insubordination in refusing the order to sign the extension letter.

In the court, Mr. Kumar claimed that he did not sign the extension letter as he was confirmed by the company before the end of his probation period. The supervisor denied that the letter he gave to Mr. Kumar was a confirmation letter. The court agreed that the letter was given to Mr. Kumar to assist him in obtaining a car loan from a financial institution. The letter was addressed to *"Kepada Sesiapa Yang Berkenaan"* (To Whom it May Concern) and it was different from the usual format of the company's Letter of Confirmation.

Refusal of Mr. Kumar to sign the extension letter amounts to an act of insubordination as the company's order for him to sign the letter was lawful. The court found that the termination of employment in this case was with just cause or excuse.

Employer's Tips

1. Make sure all orders and instructions given to the employees are lawful and reasonable.
    - The employer is not supposed to order his or her employees to do something which is illegal or dangerous.
    - The orders given to the employees must be within the terms and condition of the individual's contract of employment.
    - Give clear directions to the employees and make sure they understand the orders.
    - Find out the reasons why the employee refuses to obey his or her superior's order.
    - Assess the impact of the insubordination act.
    - Warn the employees of the disciplinary consequences if they fail to follow orders.

2. Establish whether an employee is guilty of insubordination and whether the proven insubordination constitutes to just cause or excuse for the dismissal.
    - Investigate the allegation fairly and collect all documents (e.g., emails, performance appraisals, warning letters) which may adduce evidence of insubordination.
    - Remember that the burden of proof is on the employer. The employers have to prove their case on a balance of probabilities.
    - Issue a show cause letter to call for an explanation from the employee. Set a reasonable time frame for the employee to reply.

- If there is no reply or the response is not acceptable or vague, HR may issue a Notice of Domestic Inquiry.
- Conduct the domestic inquiry in a fairly manner and make sure the employee gets an opportunity to defend himself or herself.
- The punishment given must be proportionate to the misconduct committed. The employers should take into account the employee's past records, performance levels, years of service, general behaviour, level of seniority, and the number of times the offence have occurred before giving the extreme punishment of dismissal.
- If the employee is proven guilty and the act is a very serious misconduct, the employer is entitled to terminate his or her service.

3

DISMISSAL FOR MISCONDUCT: SEXUAL HARASSMENT

No one enjoys being sexually harassed, but the victims in large tend to suffer in silence. They are ashamed to reveal their ordeal to others. Some victims are reluctant to report because they fear retaliation and loss of career opportunities. Filing a civil suit against the perpetrators is also time-consuming and costly. Most victims feel bad and are likely to quit.

For employers, sexual harassment is associated with productivity losses. It prevents employees from effectively contributing to the organisation by creating a hostile environment. Thus, employers must prevent sexual harassment and take appropriate corrective action once they come across such misconduct.

It is critical that employers and employees are familiar with what constitutes to sexual harassment in the workplace.

A Code of Practice on the Prevention and Eradication of Sexual Harassment in the Workplace was issued by the Ministry of Human Resources (MOHR) in 1999. The Code defines sexual harassment as:

Any unwanted conduct of a sexual nature, having the effect of verbal, non-verbal, visual, psychological or physical harassment:
1 that might, on reasonable grounds, be perceived by the recipient as placing a condition of a sexual nature on his or her employment; or
2 that might, on reasonable grounds, be perceived by the recipient as an offence or humiliation, or a threat to his or her well-being, but has no direct link to her/his employment.

Unfortunately, the Code is merely a guideline for employers and does not have the force of law. It is ineffective as employers are not liable to adopt a written policy on sexual harassment.

The Employment Act 1955 was amended in 2012 by inserting a new provision defining sexual harassment. It is defined as "*any unwanted conduct of a sexual nature, whether verbal, non-verbal, visual, gestural or physical, directed at a person which is offensive or humiliating or is a threat to his well being arising out of and in the course of his employment*".

Another provision (a new Section 81B) makes it mandatory for all employers to establish a procedure dealing with complaints of sexual harassment and to inquire into the complaint in a manner to be prescribed by the MOHR.

The following are various instances of sexual harassment in the workplace in Malaysia:

Claimant Wins

Case 1 : **Mohd Ridzwan Abdul Razak v Asmah Hj Mohd Nor**

Case No. : 01(f)-13-06/2013 (W)

Civil Appeal No. : W-02(NCVC)(W)-2524-10-2012

Asmah binti Hj Mohd Nor worked as a Senior Manager at Lembaga Tabung Haji attached to the Risk Management Division. Her immediate supervisor was Mohd Ridzwan bin Abdul Razak. Asmah lodged a complaint of sexual harassment against Mohd Ridzwan to the CEO. She claimed that Mohd Ridzwan uttered vulgar remarks and dirty jokes, frequently used rude and uncouth words in emails, and repeatedly invited her to be his second wife. Following an internal investigation, Mohd Ridzwan was issued a strong reprimand by the company's Human Resources Department. He was transferred to a different division of the company.

Mohd Ridzwan then proceeded to file a claim for defamation against Asmah in the High Court. Asmah in return filed her defence, detailing the vulgar words and sexually oriented statements made by Mohd Ridzwan. Relying largely on a psychiatrist's report, Asmah counterclaimed for damages predicated on sexual harassment.

On 2 June 2016, for the first time, the Malaysian High Court has awarded damages to a victim of sexual harassment in the workplace. The Federal Court dismissed

Ridzwan's lawsuit against Asmah. She was awarded RM120,000/- in damages.

The Federal Court concluded: *"Sexual harassment is a very serious misconduct and in whatever form it takes, cannot be tolerated by anyone. In whatever form it comes, it lowers the dignity and respect of the person who is harassed, let alone affecting his or her mental and emotional well-being. Perpetrators who go unpunished will continue intimating, humiliating and traumatising the victims thus resulting, at least, in an unhealthy working environment"*.

This case made a landmark decision as there is no civil cause of action for sexual harassment under the present Malaysian law. It gave room for victims who are sexually harassed in their work place to file a civil suit to claim damages against the perpetrators.

Case 2 : Mohd Nasir Deraman v Sistem Televisyen Malaysia Berhad (TV3)
Case No. : 2/4-1456/07
Award No. : 480 of 2010

Miss Ong Vincci was a practical trainee for the position of Production Assistant/Broadcasting Journalist. She made a written complaint to her supervisor and the Human Resources and Management Services of an alleged sexual harassment towards her by Mohd Nasir Deraman. He was the Executive Broadcast Journalist for TV3.

While travelling in the company car to produce a programme in Port Dickson, Mohd Nasir lay down on her lap despite her rejection. Miss Ong Vincci also stated that Mohd Nasir made suckling sounds at her and, while looking at her breast, asked her if he could bite it. She cried and was frightened. But the other two male colleagues who sat in the front seats did not do anything to stop Mohd Nasir.

The company issued a letter to show cause and suspension from work to Mohd Nasir. In his letter, he denied the allegations. He said that he was tired of driving and moved to the back seat. He laid his head on her lap after she gave him the permission.

Mohd Nasir also said that he had the habit of making sucking sounds as there was a small hole or space in between his front teeth. He denied to make such sounds with any malicious intention towards Ong Vincci. He claimed that the utterance of the words "biting of breasts" was a general joke amongst them and not directed at Ong Vincci.

The company found that his explanation was unsatisfactory and unacceptable. Therefore, the company issued a Notice of Domestic Inquiry. Mohd Nasir was dismissed from the service of the company.

The court held that, "*The claimant's defence is a bare denial of the wrongdoing and a blatant lie and not acceptable at all.*" The court stated that the act of Mohd Nasir lying on the lap of a female colleague is a deviant behaviour— regardless it was done with or without consent. Indeed, it was an act of sexual harassment and totally unacceptable.

Case 3   : Khoo Ee Peng v Galaxy Automation Sdn. Bhd.
Case No. : 9/4-2260/06
Award No. : 656 of 2009

Khoo Ee Peng was a Sales Executive at Galaxy Automation Sdn. Bhd. She reported directly to the Branch Manager, Mr. Teoh Soon Taik. Khoo filed a suit against the company for constructive dismissal and has been awarded RM16,000/- in damages by the Industrial Court.

Ms. Khoo had been employed on 15 March 2005. In her statement of claim, she said on 4 April 2005, she went to meet a customer together with Mr. Teoh in his car. After meeting with the customer, Mr. Teoh brought her to a restaurant, although she requested him to bring her back to the place where she parked her car. Around midnight, the Branch Manager drove her to a hotel and invited her to share the room with him. She rejected his advances and he sent her back eventually. On the following day, he sent an SMS declaring his love to her.

Ms. Khoo did not complain about the hotel incident to higher management because she feared of losing her job. She claimed that Mr. Teoh had tried to touch her on numerous occasions before the hotel incident. She attested that, after the incident, her petrol allowance was taken away and she was given work that she did not like.

On 21 November 2005, Ms. Khoo informed the Director of the company about the hotel incident after Mr. Teoh told her that she had been dismissed. Mr. Teoh blamed her for not filling in a leave application form on 18 November 2005. Unfortunately, the Director asked her to resign. She had no choice and proceeded to claim constructive dismissal.

Mr. Teoh did not appear at the trial. The court found that a dismissal had taken place and ordered the company to pay compensation. As Mr. Teoh had resigned from the company, the court ordered the company to reinstate Ms. Khoo to her former position without loss of seniority.

Case 4 : Encik Edwin Michael Jalleh v Freescale Semiconductor Malaysia Sdn Bhd

Case No. : 21/4-158/06
Award No. : 2160 of 2008

Mr. Edwin was a Senior Manufacturing Supervisor at an electronics factory owned by Freescale Semiconductor Malaysia Sdn. Bhd. He was dismissed for deliberately touched/patted/smacked a young female employee on her buttock. The company contended that his act was under the category of "unacceptable conduct" of the Disciplinary Policy of the company. The company adopted the Code of Practice for The Prevention and Eradication of Sexual Harassment in the Workplace.

Mr. Edwin denied the claim. After the domestic inquiry, he was dismissed. He said that he had been victimised by the Manufacturing Manager of the company who held a grudge against him.

The Industrial Court held that the act of smacking the buttocks of female employee was an act of sexual harassment. The court took into account the fact that the act occurred in an "open area" and it happened when the victim was surrounded by her colleagues. Based on the character evidence from a pastor of a church and his 28-year of service with the company, the court found that the punishment was too harsh.

The court awarded compensation in lieu of reinstatement (RM6,760/- per year x 20 years) and back wages at RM6,760/- per month for 24 months, but the amount was scaled down by 30% for his contributory misconduct.

Case 5 : Ahmad Ibrahim bin Dato Seri Mohd Ghazali v. Augustland Hotel Sdn. Bhd.

Case No. : 10(20)/4 – 1878/07
Award No. : 1460 of 2010

Ahmad Ibrahim worked in the Food & Beverages Department at Augustland Hotel since November 2000. His service was terminated in January 2007 on the grounds of sexual misconduct. He went to the Industrial Court to assert that the termination has been without just cause or excuse.

Ahmad Ibrahim was accused of sexually harassed a female cashier in the F&B Department by touching her lips and smacking her buttocks twice without her consent. During the internal investigation, the investigation officer found some doubt in the cashier's account of the incident. Ahmad Ibrahim said he previously reprimanded the cashier for being away from her workstation without permission and that led her to make false allegations against him.

The court found that no substantive and corroborated evidence of the accusation adduced at trial. The court said the termination was without just cause or excuse. Consequently, the court ordered a sum of RM33,361.55/- back wages be paid to Ahmad Ibrahim.

Employer's Tips

1. Ensure that employees understand the rules and policies of the company.
    - Make all employees aware of the company's stand on sexual harassment.
    - Have a written sexual harassment policy.
    - Provide a clear and broad statement defining what constitutes sexual harassment.
    - Effective training to teach employees about what is and isn't acceptable workplace behaviours.
    - Specify that offenders will be subjected to appropriate disciplinary actions.

2. Establish procedures to handle complaints about sexual harassment.
    - Set up a list of names together with their designations to whom complaints can be made.
    - State that employees who experience or witness harassment are required to report it.
    - Inquire into all complaints of sexual harassment in a manner prescribed by the Minister of Human Resources [Employment Act 1955 section 81B (1)].
    - The employer must inform complainants of their refusal to inquire into the complaint of sexual harassment, as soon as practicable, but no later than 30 days after the date of the receipt of the complaint, and reason for refusal (section 81B (2) of Employment Act 1955).
    - The employer may decline to inquire into the complaint in two situations: (1) if the complaint

has previously been inquired into and no sexual harassment has been proven; or (2) if the employer is of the opinion that the complaint of sexual harassment is frivolous, vexatious or is not made in good faith (section 81B (3) of Employment Act 1955).
- An employee who is not satisfied with the refusal of the employer to inquire may refer the matter to the Director General of Labour. The employer must inquire into complaints if directed to do so by the Director General. (section 81B (4) and (5) of Employment Act 1955).
- The employer must submit a report of the enquiry into sexual harassment to the Director General.

3. Provide protection to those involved in the sexual harassment investigations.
    - Give the person accused of harassment the opportunity to respond immediately after complaints are made.
    - Confidentiality should be kept where possible to encourage reporting.
    - Assure employees that they won't be subjected to retaliation for reporting incidents of sexual harassment.

4. Provide a fair system for discipline and punishment.
    - If, upon conducting an inquiry, the employer is satisfied that sexual harassment is proven, disciplinary actions may be taken against the employee: dismissing without notice, downgrading

or imposing any other lesser punishment which the employer deems just and fit (section. 81B (1) (a) of Employment Act 1955).

- If an employer imposes the punishment of suspension without wages, it shall not exceed 2 weeks (section. 81B (1) (a) (iii) of Employment Act 1955).

4

TERMINATION OF PROBATIONERS

New recruits are usually placed on probation to test their suitability for employment. The Employment Act 1955 does not have any clause that specifies the probation period. Nevertheless, the most common period for a probation is 1, 3 and 6 months. The employer will be able to gauge the job performance, character and attitude of the employee during the probation period. In some instances, the employer may extend the probationary period to give an opportunity for the probationer to improve his or her performance.

If the employer does not terminate the service of the employee or confirm the employee after the stipulated probation period, an employee appointed on probation remains a probationer unless it is stated otherwise in the employment letter where confirmation is automatic unless stated otherwise before the end of the probation period.

It was held in the case of Azmi & Company Sdn Bhd v Firdaus Musa that:

"Employee cannot assume confirmation in the absence of express confirmation from his employer. Until he is expressly confirmed and if no action is taken by the employer either by way of confirmation or by way of termination, he is assumed to continue in service as a probationer."

However, when the employer treats the probationer as he or she was a confirmed staff and the employee receives benefits to which only confirmed staff are entitled, the employee shall be deemed to have been confirmed in his service.

Can a probationer be dismissed before the end of his or her probationary period? In the case of Khaliah Abbas v Pesaka Capital Corporation Sdn Bhd [1997], the Court of Appeal has propounded the following:

"It is our view that an employee on probation enjoys the same rights as a permanent or confirmed employee and his or her services cannot be terminated without just cause or excuse. The requirement of bona fide is essential in the dismissal of an employee on probation, but if the dismissal or termination is found to be a colourable exercise of the power to dismiss or as a result of discrimination or unfair labour practice, the Industrial Court has the jurisdiction to interfere and to set aside such dismissal."

Employees on probation are allowed to enjoy the same minimum entitlements as those who are not on probation.

Hence, in the event that the employer is unsatisfied with the performance of an employee on probation, the employer may terminate the services of the employee, but care must be taken by the employer where proper procedures must be followed prior to dismissal. An employee cannot be terminated without cause or excuse. A probationer can be dismissed during the probation period for a good cause, such as misconduct or redundancy, after a proper inquiry has been held. But if a probationer claimed that the dismissal was unfair, he or she can lodge a claim under section 20 of the Industrial Act 1967 for reinstatement. If an employer is found guilty of firing a probationer without just cause, a probationer is entitled to compensation in lieu of reinstatement to a maximum of 12 months of the employee's last drawn salary.

Grounds for Lawsuit against Employer

Case 1 : Indra Devi a/p Rajoo v. Everhome Furniture Mfr (M) Sdn. Bhd.

Case No. : 12(14)/4-391/11
Award No. : 93 of 2015

Human Resource Junior Executive, Indra Devi, was appointed for a 3-month probationary period, with a monthly salary of RM1,200/-. Her service was terminated approximately after 11 months in service on the grounds of unsatisfactory performance. She was accused of having poor attitudes and making many mistakes in her duties.

The court found that the company, Everhome Furniture Mfr (M) Sdn. Bhd. failed to produce any documentary evidence such as warning letters, memos or reminders to her about the unsatisfactory performance. She was only given training in the first month of her appointment and no proper guidance and further training was given during her service in the company. Besides, no formal performance appraisal was carried out by the management of the company on Indra Devi.

The court found that the dismissal was without just cause or excuse and ordered five months back wages to be paid to Indra Devi.

Case 2   : Lee Pei Sze v. Swiftlet Garden Sdn. Bhd.
Case No.   : 16/4-664/16
Award No. : 167 of 2017

Ms. Lee Pei Sze was hired an Account Executive position at Swiflet Garden Sdn. Bhd. Upon being dismissed from her position during the probation period, she claimed reinstatement under section 20, Industrial Act 1967.

Ms. Lee received a termination letter from the company, but the letter did not state the reason for termination. Besides, she claimed that no formal performance review and domestic inquiry was conducted by the company prior dismissal. Thus, she alleged that her dismissal was without just cause or excuse.

The company accused her for failing to show up at work on time despite various reminders and verbal warnings given to her. The company asserted that the dismissal was fair as the company has paid RM4,500/- being compensated to Ms. Lee in lieu of one-month notice.

The court concluded that the allegation against Ms. Lee was as it lacked material particulars. The company failed to particularise those allegations. The court found that Ms. Lee was dismissed without just cause or excuse. Under the Second Schedule of the Industrial Relations Act 1967, a probationer is only entitled to back wages and not entitled to reinstatement. Thus, the court directed the company to pay RM19,500/- of back wages to Ms. Lee.

The Employer Wins

Case 3 : Tan Cheng Leng v Tropicana Medical Centre (M) Sdn Bhd

Case No. : 2/4-15/15
Award No. : 159 of 2017

Mr. Tan was appointed as an Account Executive by Tropicana Medical Centre (M) Sdn Bhd. After a review on his performance by his superior during his 3-month probation period, the company decided to extend his probation period for another three months. His service was terminated before the end of the extended probation period on the grounds of unsatisfactory performance and disciplinary record.

Mr. Tan contended that his dismissal had been without just cause and excuse and that he had been bullied and victimised by his immediate supervisor.

The court found that he has been informed and advised of his poor performance after the first appraisal. Unfortunately, Mr. Tan showed little improvement in his attitudes and work performance during the extended probationary period. A show cause letter was issued to him with regards to his misconduct in taking leave without prior approval and came in late to work without reason.

The court observed from the attendance record that Mr. Tan was in the habit of defying simple instructions and policies such as having to clock in and out. Also, the email communication between Mr. Tan and his supervisor clearly showed he was not committed in his duties and refused to follow the company's policy.

Hence, the court found that the termination was for a just cause or excuse.

Case 4 : **Hari Bala A/L R. Parasuraman v. Johnson Control (M) Sdn. Bhd.**

Case No. : 3/4-1299/06
Award No. : 1390 of 2009

Hari Bala, a field engineer at Johnson Control (M) Sdn. Bhd., was dismissed at the end of his extended probation period. His supervisor, Mr. Mohan, conducted a performance review on him prior to the termination. Mr. Mohan pointed out three areas of improvement required from Hari Bala and gave poor ratings for him in the Progress Review Report. The report was signed by Mr. Mohan and Hari Bala.

Sarah Tan, Human Resources Officer, testified that she had a meeting with Mr. Mohan and Hari Bala to discuss the matter. She recalled that Hari Bala was reluctant to improve in those areas identified by Mr. Mohan and he claimed that they were not part of his job.

The court pointed out that Mr. Mohan is the best person to evaluate Hari Bala's performance and found that Hari Bala was dismissed with just cause and excuse.

Case 5 : **Azizah Binti Ahmad v Malayan Banking Berhad**

Case No. : 2/4-429/12

Award No. : 476 of 2017

Puan Azizah was appointed as Head Merchant Portfolio Management at Malayan Banking Berhad on a 6-month probation period, with a monthly salary of RM4,500/-. Her service was terminated nine months after she started working. She was terminated on the grounds of unsatisfactory performance. However, she claimed that her dismissal was done without any performance review, work evaluation, appraisal or any warning letter for improvement.

When her probation period expired, the bank extended her probation period for another 3-month as she was on medical leave for 52 days before the end of the probation period. The court found that Puan Azizah left the medical leave certificates on her supervisor's in-tray at odd hours and day.

Her supervisor decided not to confirm her service as she took 117 days of medical leave. Furthermore, she recommended for non-confirmation as Puan Azizah did not perform well in the projects given to her prior to her absence.

Although there are no warning letters or verbal warnings provided to Puan Azizah, the court concluded that her dismissal was carried out with just cause or excuse. The court decided that there is no need for a formal written warning since Puan Azizah is not a junior staff who needs directions on the job. Besides, she failed to return to work after the extended probationary period.

Employer's Tips

1. An employer must be very careful before hiring an employee and should always conduct reference checks.
   - An employee on probation has the same rights as a permanent or confirmed employee and cannot be dismissed without just cause or excuse.
   - The service of a probationer can only be terminated on the grounds of misconduct, poor performance or redundancy.
   - A probationer has a right to make a representation to the Director-General of Industrial Relations under section 20 of the Industrial Relations Act 1967 for unfair dismissal.
   - A probationer is entitled to compensation in lieu of reinstatement to a maximum of 12 months' back wages based on the last drawn salary if the court finds that the dismissal was without just cause and excuse.

2. At the end of the probationary period, the employer should notify the employee whether he or she has been confirmed, unconfirmed, or the probation period is being extended.
   - An employee appointed on probation continues as a probationer even after the period of probation, if at the end of the period his or her services had either not been confirmed or unconfirmed.
   - An employer can evaluate and test whether the probationer possesses the right skill, competence,

temperament, aptitude, attitude and suitability prior to confirmation of employment.
- Confirmation can be implied by conduct. When the employer treats the employee as if he or she is a permanent staff (for example, the probationer received the same benefits to which permanent staff are entitled).
- A probationer will be deemed to be confirmed upon expiry of the probationary period when the contract terms state that he or she will be confirmed if no actions were taken by the employer.

3. Prior to terminating a probationer's employment, the employer should follow the following steps:
- Give warnings to the probationer about his or her unsatisfactory performance.
- Give sufficient opportunity to the probationer to improve on his or her performance, such as laying out areas of improvement, extending the probation period, and so on
- Conduct a formal performance appraisal on the probationer. The evaluation process must be documented and signed off by the probationer.
- Provide appropriate training and sufficient guidance during the probation period.

5

POOR PERFORMANCE

Unsatisfactory job performance refers to a gap between an employee's actual performance and the level of performance required by the organisation. Ability to manage employee performance is crucial as it affects organisational performance. Prior to fixing poor performance, understanding the cause is important. Was it due to can't do or won't do? The distinction is important as the type of intervention is different.

Grounds for Lawsuit against Employer

Case 1 : Raja Azmil Bin Raja Hussein v CIMB Bank Berhad

Case No. : 3(5)(25)(5)/4-453/12
Award No. : 903 of 2017

The court held that the dismissal of Raja Azmil by CIMB was without just cause or excuse based on the following points and awarded the claimant with a payment amounted to RM363,091.60 before the statutory deduction:

a. The claimant had continued to strive harder despite not meeting the KPIs and his efforts were recognised by his superiors' positive and encouraging remarks.
b. The target set by the company was unrealistic and this was supported by the bank's action in reducing the KPIs.
c. The claimant was never placed under the Performance Improvement Plan (PIP).
d. It was an unfair labour practice by the bank as claimant was dismissed for poor performance, but retained others who did not meet their KPIs.
e. The claimant was better and more knowledgeable in branch operations as compared to retail collection, and his contribution as a branch officer had been recognised by the bank via an award with the highest number of products sold for consumer loans in 2003.

Case 2   : **Yong Mee King v Kasyaf Bina Sdn Bhd**
Case No.   : 3(28)/4-1836/12
Award No. : 227 of 2015

The case of Yong Mee King and Kasyaf Bina Sdn Bhd is about termination due to poor performance. Yong Mee King, the claimant has been a Purchasing Executive since 3 March 2010 with a monthly salary plus fixed allowance of RM4,600/-. The claimant was terminated with 24 hours notice and a cheque amounting to RM4,770.75, in which she did not accept. There were three reasons for the termination. (1) Unsatisfactory performance as Purchasing Executive, (2) careless in buying inventory for and on behalf of Kasyaf Bina, which caused losses to the company and (3) influencing other employees to act against the company.

There were four evidences from this case:
1. All purchases made were requests from the company. Ms Yong was only responsible for taking orders based on the request that she had received. She also had three quotations for every intent to purchase. The managing director had approved all purchases.
2. There was no proof that Ms Yong had been negligent, committed breach of trust nor deceived the company as claimed. All purchases were approved by the company.
3. There was also no evidence from the company's staff to support the defamatory remarks made by Ms Yong as claimed by the company.

4. The company had failed to prove that her performance was below expectations. No warning, nor counselling was done. She was instead given one month's bonus after being with the company for a year, but the company claimed that it was for her delivery which the court finds it is difficult to believe. The company claimed that other employees were paid higher bonuses, but failed to bring in any evidence.

Ms. Yong won the case and the company was asked to pay back wages (basic pay and fixed allowances) for 9 months (RM5,012/- x 9 months = RM45,108/-) and compensation in lieu of reinstatement (RM5,012/- x 1 month = RM5,012/-). Total payout was RM50,120/-.

Case 3 **: Raffan Kashoggi Bin Ramli v Nectar Agro (M) Sdn. Bhd.**

Case No. : 1/1-73/17
Award No. : 929 of 2017

The claimant, Raffan Kashoggi bin Ramli was appointed as a Sales Executive at the respondent's company, Nectar Agro (M) Sdn. Bhd. on 25 October 2010 with a monthly basic salary of RM2,200/- and a monthly vehicle allowance of RM500/-. His last drawn was RM2,500/- a month. On 27 April 2012, the claimant received the following letter of termination:

> Dear Mr. Raftan:
>
> I am writing to you about termination of your employment with Nectar Agro (M) Sdn Bhd.
>
> Based on your length of service, your notice period is one month. Therefore your employment will end on 25th May 2012. We will waive your personal loan but you won't qualify for payment in May.
>
> Despite verbal and written warnings about your performance, you have not obtained the performance objectives we set on 25th October 2010.
>
> In lieu of receiving as part of your separation from Nectar Agro (M) Sdn Bhd and per company policy, we will be providing you with one month pay. Please also note that all other benefits will end on the termination date including your health and dental insurance. Please contact the health insurance company directly for information.

Encik Mohd Tamizi bin Abdullah, the only witness from the respondent (COW) claimed that a sales target was set for the claimant. There was a drop in claimant's performance as he often took sick leave. A discussion took place between him and the claimant in March 2012 where the claimant mentioned that he had personal problems and took a RM6,000/- loan from the respondent. Nevertheless, COW claimed that the claimant's performance did not change despite many repeated reminders and advice, which eventually led to the termination on 25 May 2012.

However, according to the claimant, the respondent terminated his service on the grounds that the claimant had failed to achieve the sales target set, on 25 October 2010. The claimant did not agree to the target as these were not specified in his employment letter. He also stated that he had never received any verbal nor written warning and there was no performance appraisal carried out throughout his tenure with the company.

The court found that the proof on the claimant's performance is weak. The respondent failed to provide any evidence to prove the poor performance of the claimant. The court ruled that the respondent failed to take action to warn or guide the claimant prior to the termination. Hence, the termination of claimant was without cause and excuse. The claimant was awarded RM32,500/- (Back wages: RM2,500/- x 12 months = RM30,000/- and compensation taken back to work: RM2,500/- x 1 = RM2,500/-.

Case 4 **: Hasdie Bin Tusin Against Kudat Golf v Marina Resort (Tangamahir Sdn Bhd)**

Case No. : 17/4-800/15

Award No. : 1133 of 2016

Hasdie Bin Tusin was employed by Kudat Golf & Marina Resort (Tangamahir Sdn Bhd) as a waiter cum bar tender on 15 December 2006. On 4 May 2010, he was transferred to the Front Office Department as a bell boy cum driver as per his request. The company issued 3 warning letters to the him for various misconduct which resulted in his dismissal on 9 May 2015:

- The 1st warning letter issued on 17 April 2005: Insubordination or disobedience to the orders of his superior officer, the Operating Manager, Sainin A. Momen to send him to Kota Kinabalu.
- The 2nd warning letter issued on 27 April 2005: Participated in an illegal strike, abetting and inciting others to strike and a letter with the caption "tempoh pemerhatian selama 2 bulan" [2 months' observation period] issued on 27 April 2005: His performance was below expectation and gave him 2 months to improve, failing which he would be dismissed.
- The 3rd warning letter issued on 9 May 2015: Riotous, disorderly or indecent behaviour, violence, abusing, assaulting or threatening to assault, injure or harm other employees or superiors in the company.

Hasdie Bin Tusin contends that his dismissal by the company was without just cause or excuse due to the following 5 reasons:
1. There were no specific charges of misconduct against him.
2. The 3 warning letters lack details.
3. The claimant had been punished for alleged charges before receiving the warning letters.
4. The true reason for the termination is based on the alleged non improvement in his performance.
5. The company failed to pay the claimant's minimum wage under the Minimum Wages Order 2012. His last drawn salary was RM610/-

The company failed to provide evidence of the indecent behaviour, violence, abusing and threatening other employees or superior. In the case of Intrakota Consolidated Bhd v Mohammad Roslin Md Shah & Anor 2008, where the learned judge held that the particulars such as time, place, and identity of the person in charge were essential to enable the employee to know with certainty the charge levelled against him and to allow him to prepare and conduct his defence. Since the company failed to provide sufficient evidence to support, the judge held that the claimant's dismissal was without just cause or excuse.

The claimant was awarded back wages and compensation in lieu of reinstatement of RM15,920/-.

The Employer Wins

Case 5 : **Norhayati Binti Sulaiman v Shell Malaysia Limited**

Case No. : 3 (15)/4 – 1123/15

Award No. : 1320 of 2018

The claimant was appointed as a Media Relation Manager in August 2012 under a 12-month probationary period. However, her performance rating for the year 2012 and 2013 were below expectation. She went through the Performance Improvement Plan (PIP) in the middle of 2014. By the end of 2014, the PIP results were unsatisfactory and she was terminated.

Throughout her employment with Shell, the claimant did not receive any confirmation letter but she claimed that she has been confirmed and denied that she was a poor performer as she was given a performance bonus and increment in 2012 and 2013. Besides, the claimant also claimed that she had contributed to the increased CARMA Score for the media coverage in Malaysia in 2014 and managed to publish three (3) stories in the media which exceeded her one (1) story target. However, Shell explained that the claimant was not the sole contributor to the improved CARMA Score.

The company also accused the claimant for terminating the contract with one of the suppliers, iSentia without official approval, thus jeopardising the company's relationship with the external parties. The claimant disputed that the termination was guided by her superior. Shell had also arranged for the claimant to meet a mentor from the Philippines during her PIP period. However, claimant did not cooperate and follow up on the actions agreed nor respond to the mentor. The claimant claimed that the session was a simple discussion on media and internal communication issues of less than an hour.

From the company's point of view, the claimant was a probationer and not a confirmed employee as there was no official letter nor verbal confirmation of service. Therefore, it is not an issue for them to terminate her due to incompetence.

On the other hand, from the claimant's point of view, she is a confirmed employee as her probation period has long lapsed and she was given increment and performance bonuses in 2013 and 2014, benefits that were given to employees who have been confirmed with the company. Furthermore, she was compensated 3 months of her basic salary, benefits given to employees who have been confirmed.

The court agreed with the company's decision to terminate the claimant's services due to poor performance rather than non-confirmation. The court also found that there was no evidence actuated by mala fide or act of victimisation directed against the claimant. With regards to the allegation of iSentia's contract, the court is aware that no a show cause letter issued. The claimant's dismissal has been therefore just.

Employer's Tips and Recommendations

With reference to the case, Goodway Rubber Industries Sdn Bhd. v Charles James Henry George [2003] 1 ILR 279 where it states that, in dealing with dismissal cases where poor performance has been alleged:
i) Employee must be warned about his or her poor performance;
ii) Employee must be given sufficient time and opportunity to improve and
iii) Employee fails to improve his or her performance after the sufficient time given.

In short, proper documentation is a must. Evidence must be gathered to support any statement given. The company cannot dismiss an employee without any proof. The employee must be told of his or her poor performance in advance. Employers should place poor performers under the performance improvement plan where expected improvement and deadlines to achieve must be clearly stated and understood by the employee. The employee should also be given sufficient time and opportunity to improve. Lastly, a company should not state bonus if it is for delivery.

It is important to have proper documentation with fair performance appraisal system. It is always a good practice to give under performers a chance to improve their performance. Employers need to prove that employees are aware of their weaknesses. Sufficient training and guidance must be given to equip the employees with the skills and knowledge to perform the assigned tasks.

Despite such efforts by the employer and the employee's performance is still unsatisfactory, the employer must:

- Warn the employee about his or her poor performance.
- That the employee was accorded sufficient opportunity to improve.
- The employee has failed to improve his or her performance.

6

REDUNDANCY

Redundancy occurs when a person's post becomes unnecessary. Possible situation that could lead to redundancy is business restructuring where a surplus of labour could be reduced.

In most instances, Human Resource will redeploy the employee to another job whenever possible or offer a compensation package to employees as a form of assistance to them for their loss of income and to make up for this unfortunate state. The company would usually also take accountability on the employability of the laid-off employee by making sure they are able to obtain any employment in the future through good references and recommendations.

Grounds for Lawsuit against Employer

Case 1 : **Mariana Binti Hassan v British American Tobacco (Malaysia) Berhad**

Case No. : 26/4-730/06
Award No. : 781 of 2008

The claimant started her employment as a Data Entry Operator on 1 April 1990. In 2001, the company has decided to outsource its Helpdesk services. On 22 February 2001, the claimant was called into the IT meeting room and was offered three documents: Voluntary Separation Scheme (VSS), Employment Separation Scheme and a 3-month job contract. The company did not allow Mariana to leave the room, nor give sufficient time for the claimant to think about the offer. If the claimant refused to sign the VSS offered by the company, she would be terminated without any compensation and would not be able to work with the company for another three months. Hence, she ended her employment with the company due to pressure and she signed the VSS on 22 February 2001.

The court found that the retrenchment was not done fairly and the dismissal is without just cause or excuse. The court then awarded compensation in lieu of reinstatement for each completed year of service and back wages for the duration where the claimant was unemployed subject to a maximum of 24 months.

- Back wages: RM2,573/- (last drawn) x 24 months = RM61,752/-

- Compensation in lieu of reinstatement: RM54,194/- (after deducting RM51,299/- from RM105,493/- that had been already paid to the claimant as compensation).

Case 2 : **Kuldip Singh A/L Sarban Singh v Ismeca Malaysia Sdn. Bhd. (IMAL).**
Case No. : 11/4 – 62/11
Award No. : 553 of 2015

The claimant commenced employment as a Supply Chain Manager for Malaysia on 23 October 2007 with a basic salary of RM16,001/- per month plus RM400/- monthly travelling allowance. The claimant was confirmed on 22 April 2008, after six months of probation. In less than 5 months, on 1 September 2008, the claimant was promoted to a Global Supply Chain Manager with a monthly salary of RM19,801/-, as the headquarter was relocated to IMAL from Switzerland. The decision to relocate the headquarter was done by Peter Portmann, the Vice-President of Global or World Wide Operations for Ismeca Semiconductor. On 22 October 2010 before lunch, the claimant was called for a meeting with Peter Portmann, Ng Yu Ting (IMAL President), and the Finance and Human Resource Manager (company's witness, COW1). In the meeting, the claimant was informed that his position became redundant due to the relocation of Global Supply Chain Management (GSCM) Department to Switzerland. He was given two options to choose. (1) To voluntarily resign. (2) His employment will be terminated. Whichever option the claimant chooses, he will be compensated for his 2.5 years of service with RM82.860.21.

After the meeting, the claimant informed the management of his decision of not resigning. At 4:00 pm on the same day, the claimant's email was cut off. At 6:00 pm, the company handed the claimant a termination of employment agreement and pressured the claimant to sign it. Upon signing, he was escorted out of the premise. The claimant also mentioned that on the day itself, his subordinates were briefed on his termination. He also highlighted in court that all the suppliers were informed of this decision and were advised to direct all correspondence to Thierry Perrot, the acting Malaysia Supply Chain Manager.

The claimant highlighted that he held dual role, as Global Supply Chain Manager and also as Supply Chain Manager for IMAL. Therefore, if the position of GSCM position was redundant due to relocation, the Supply Chain Manager (SCM) position for IMAL is still available. However, from the company's point of view, it was a different issue. They mentioned that the claimant was promoted to GSCM manager and there was no dual role.

The court found that there was no option given to the claimant. The claimant would be terminated even if he did not want to resign. Hence, this was a dismissal. On the nature of the dismissal, the justification given by the company was redundancy as a result of relocation. The court finds that it only affects the GSCM position and not SCM position. The function of IMAL SCM remained in Malaysia. This was proven when the company advertised for the SCM post for IMAL. The claimant wrote in for the position after seeing the advertisement in April 2011. However, the position was filled by Mr. Giam Boon Pin. This proved that the relocation of the Global Supply

Chain department did not result in a surplus of labour and there was no redundancy for the SCM position.

Another issue was about the claimant's retirement age. According to the company handbook, the retirement age was 55. The claimant was 55 in 2010. However, there was a clause in the claimant's appointment letter that states:

"Special Condition: As per special arrangement, you shall continue to serve the company after the retirement age of 55 years (based on Ismeca Malaysia official retirement age) which will not be on the restriction of Malaysian Government Law."

Hence, this clause overrides the company handbook and therefore the claimant was entitled to compensation in lieu of reinstatement.

The award decided by the court was that the company is to pay the claimant 2¼ months' salary, i.e. one month for each year of service. Claimant's last drawn before dismissal as GSCM was RM19,801/-. Therefore, the total compensation in lieu of reinstatement was RM44,552.25. The court also decided that the claimant was to be paid back wages equivalent of 16 months' salary which came up to RM318.816/-. Hence, the total compensation to be paid to the claimant was RM361,368.25. The amount that was paid to the claimant upon dismissal was RM82,860.21. Upon deduction of the amount, the company had to pay the claimant an additional RM278,508.04.

The Employer Wins

Case 3 : Suzielly Sheilly Bt. Z Mambang v LF Asia Sebor (Sabah) Holdings Sdn. Bhd.

Case No. : 17/4-1249/15
Award No. : 212 of 2017

The claimant was appointed as an Operator Grade C stationed at the company's warehouse in Kota Kinabalu. On 1 March 2015, the company gave her 2 months' termination notice due to warehouse operations downsizing as the company has lost its distributorships and the company followed the industrial principle of "last in, first out". She claimed that the company wanted to terminate her and to replace her with their choice of candidate. She also contended that she was dismissed without just cause or excuse based on the final reminder and final warning due to her history of reporting late for work and taking leave without obtaining proper approval from the company.

The court contended that the company had made reasonable and appropriate decision with regards to redundancy and financial status at the material time. The court also found that in order to do a Proof of Delivery, one must be computer literate and trained in the Company's Warehouse Management System. Also, the court found that the company did not take any action against her after the final reminder and final warning. This indicates that such allegation is misplaced and unsubstantiated.

Hence, the court found that the retrenchment was reasonable and proper.

Case 4   : Syd Hashim Bin Syed Othman v Ismeca Malaysia Sdn. Bhd

Case no.   : 15/4 – 1587/12
Award No. : 399/2015

IMAL was involved in a similar dismissal case of Syed Hashim bin Syed Othman. However, in this case, IMAL managed to prove that the claimant's unit was closed down due to poor business order, thus there was a surplus of employees. The company also managed to justify why the particular department was closed down.

Case 5 : **Vijayakumar A/L K. Bathumalai v Inter Data Technologies (Malaysia) Sdn. Bhd.**

Case No. : 14/4 - 488/01

Award No. : 937 of 2003

The claimant, Vijayakumar A/L K. Bathumalai was dismissed by way of retrenchment as a result of redundancy. The claimant started working with the company on 1 July 1987 as an Accounts Clerk. Thereafter, the company was known as Toppan Moore Paragon (Malaysia) Sdn. Bhd. On 1 September 1990, he was promoted to a Shipping Officer. On 1 June 1998, the claimant was terminated. His last drawn was RM2,480/- and RM300/- as his monthly travelling allowance. The claimant claimed that the dismissal was without cause or excuse.

The company claimed that the claimant's termination was due to the reduction of his core responsibilities. Besides, the company also claimed that overall profitability does not allow them to absorb any additional manpower into any branch nor division within the company. Hence, the claimant was dismissed with just cause or excuse.

The court was satisfied with the evidences and found that the claimant had been dismissed with just cause or excuse.

Employer's Tips

Redundancy should be managed effectively. Some of the ways to manage redundancy are as follows:
- Consider all alternatives such as transferring, reducing or freezing employees' salaries or bonuses.
- Keep communication open on redundancy.
- Offer relevant programme for employee to prepare them for a new job.

Employers have the right to relocate the business and reorganise for the betterment of the organisation. However, the relocation/reorganisation must be genuine, sufficient notice should be given to the employees and cannot be done with the intention to terminate an employee. If an employee's service is terminated due to the relocation, the employer needs to proof that the relocation has caused redundancy of the particular position. The company also needs to justify why the employee could not be transferred to another department or to another branch with same/similar job function. As in the earlier case, the company was not able to provide evidence for any of the above, and moreover, the company conducted recruitment, the court concluded that the dismissal was unfair and unjust to the interest of the claimant.

Next, the retirement age clause in the employment letter should be standardised for all employees. Any extension of employment beyond retirement age should be done via yearly contract. By doing this, the company has more control on the employment of employees above retirement age. In additional to this, companies should also refer to the Code of Conduct for Industrial Harmony 1975.

7
RETRENCHMENT

Retrenchment is derived from a French word, retrancher which means cut down or cut short. Retrenchment/laid off are often, but may not be the result of poor economy. Nevertheless, it is commonly understood as being part of business strategy in handling business losses. Companies in general are allowed to organise their business in a manner that best achieves their objectives in making profit so long as it is is bona fide. When a company suffers losses, companies should follow through The Code of Conduct for Industrial Harmony ("Code"), may terminate some employees or outsource some functions.

Grounds for Lawsuit against Employer

Case 1 : **Maimunah Binti Daud & 8 Others v GG Timur Trading**
Case No. : 18(12)/4-1075/15
Award No. : 658 of 2017

The 9 plaintiffs were appointed as cleaners by the company without any letter of appointment. The plaintiffs were Maimunah binti Daud, Ma Kalthom binti Daud, Seripah binti Abdul Rahman, Rahimah binti Awang, Suriyani binti Manaf, Nor Anita bint Taha, Roslina binti Mohd Noor, Siti Fatimah binti Ag Ngah and Noraini binti Yahya. Their duration of service ranged from 6 months to 2 year 3 months. On 13 April 2015, GG Timur Trading issued them notice of service termination at SMK Seri Nering without any reason.

Prior to the termination, their salaries were RM900/- per month with the exception of Noraini binti Yahya, where her last drawn was RM630/- per month and they had payslips to prove that they were employees of GG Timur Trading. Ex-parte trial was held as the company was not present. Hence, based on available evidence from the plaintiffs, the court contended that GG Timur Trading had dismissed their employees without just cause and excuses. GG Timur Trading had to pay a range of 3 to 5 months of salaries to the 9 plaintiffs, based on their earlier agreed tenure (duration of service) and some of them were unemployed till 1 January 2016.

Case 2 : Maser Sdn. Bhd. v. Yeoh Oon Wah
Case No. : 1:4/4-95/88
Award No. : 241 of 1990

Mr Yeoh Oon Wah, the plaintiff was a Sales Manager attached to Pumps Division at Maser Sdn. Bhd since 18 September 1985. He was terminated by the company on 7 May 1987 after 1 year and 6 months as the company claimed that it was due to economic slowdown.

The termination letter did not disclose any reason for termination. Economy condition was not the reason for termination as the company was in the midst of proposing to diversify and enlarge the Pumps Division where two positions were advertised for the Pumps Division (1) Sale Manager and (2) Sales Engineer after the termination. No obvious evidence was provided to support the company's losses.

In addition to the above, during the cross-examination, the plaintiff claimed that he had an argument with the Managing Director in February 1987 and the court has faith that this was associated with the issuance of the memoranda to the plaintiff on 27 February and 6 April of the same year. From all the evidences provided by both the plaintiff and defendant, the court held that the company had established mala fide and the termination of the plaintiff's employment services was a disguised dismissal effected without just cause or excuse.

The court decided on the following:

(1) Back wages:
- The plaintiff's last drawn salary was RM2,500/- per month.
- Contractual allowance was RM200/- per month.
- Total income earned was RM2,700/- per month.
- The plaintiff's last day of service was on 7 May 1987.
- The case hearing in April and July 1990, a lapse of approximately 3 years. However, the court only permits a maximum period of 24 months (2 years) in accordance with the practice.
- Hence, the back wages were RM2,700/- x 24 = RM64,800/-.

(2) Compensation in lieu of reinstatement: RM2,700/- x 3 years = RM8,100/-.

(3) The court had also taken into consideration that the plaintiff had some behavioural problems towards his superiors. The two memoranda given to the plaintiff were to warn him to improve his behaviour, but there was no feedback from the plaintiff. For this reason, the court allowed a 30% deduction from the total amount of RM72,900/-, a slash of RM21,870/-. Hence, the final total amount awarded to the plaintiff was RM51,030/, which shall be paid by the company to the plaintiff within one (1) month subject to the usual tax deductions and Employee' Provident Fund contribution if any.

The Employer Wins

Case 3 : Vijayakumar A/L K. Bathumalai vs Inter Data Technologies (Malaysia) Sdn. Bhd.

Case No. : 14/4 - 488/01
Award No. : 937 of 2003

The claimant, Vijayakumar A/L K. Bathumalai was retrenched as a result of redundancy. The claimant started working with the company on 1 July 1987 as an Accounts Clerk and was promoted to a Shipping Officer on 1 September 1990. The company terminated the claimant on 1 June 1998. At the time of termination, his basic salary was RM2,480/- plus a monthly travelling allowance of RM300/-. The claimant claimed that the dismissal was without cause or excuse.

On the other hand, the company claimed that the claimant's termination was necessary as there was a reduction in his core responsibilities (Procurement Department). Besides, the company also claimed that overall profit dropped and unable to absorb any surplus of workers to other branches or divisions as well. The company declared that the claimant was dismissed with just cause or excuse.

The court was satisfied with the evidences. It is clear that there was a severe 60.3% reduction or shrinkage of the claimant's job. Hence, the company has the right to close down the Shipping/Procurement Department and terminate the claimant as the claimant's job had become redundant. In addition to that, the court also found that due to the economic downturn, the company's sales volume has dropped drastically. The company also suffered financial losses and the number of staff was reduced from 200 to 98. Hence, the claimant had been dismissed with just cause or excuse.

Case 4 : Vijayapal Singh A/L Hira Singh v Kelab Sukan Pulau Pinang

Case No. : 11(9)/4-509/14
Award No. : 1141 of 2017

This case was divided into two parts. (1) Retrenchment on the 1 October 1989 and (2) termination on 28 February 1999.

Retrenchment on 1 October 1989: The claimant was retrenched on 1 October 1989 as the restaurant and bar were running at a loss. However, the claimant was unhappy with the retrenchment and lodged a complaint with the Industrial Relation Department for conciliation but failed. He was then referred to the Industrial Court for adjudication and that was after the restaurant was privatised. He was reinstated on 23 December 1994. After the reinstatement, he filed an appeal against the decision of the Industrial Court to the High Court but was unsuccessful. A new position was created for the claimant as the company was no longer running the restaurant. It was created out of goodwill and compassion. It did not constitute to a fresh employment. Not satisfied with the decision, he appealed to the Court of Appeal. The company was not obliged to let the claimant to continue working because the Court of Appeal's decision had concluded that the retrenchment was justified.

Termination on 28 February 1999: Despite being retrenched, the claimant continued working and draw a salary from the company. The company asked the claimant to comply with the Court of Appeal and to cease work from 28 February 1999. The claimant's position was not filled after the claimant left the company.

In May 1985, the claimant joined the company as a Bar Captain. On 1 December 1997, the company sent a letter that assured his current position even though there was a change in management. Six days later, the claimant wrote a letter stating that he did not understand the content of that letter but there was no reply. On 28 February 1999, the claimant was dismissed from the company. The claimant disagreed with the sudden dismissal and referred to his letter dated 6 December 1997. The claimant claimed that the company had assured his position to work with the company until the application to the Federal Court is disposed of and Federal Court has yet to dispose the application at the time of dismissal. The claimant lodged a complaint to the Ministry of Human Resource, but was rejected. The claimant then filed an appeal to the High Court, and succeeded.

On 28 February 1999, the claimant was officially terminated from his service. During cross-examination, the witness stated that the claimant only ceased from work and not retrenched. However, it was later revised and edited. It was later confirmed that the claimant was retrenched. The claimant agreed that he was retrenched for the second time, but he disagreed with the condition put by the company. He said that he did not know about the condition. The counsel for the claimant said that it was an afterthought of the company when making the decision to retrench him. Also, the claimant had appeal for leave at the federal court and the company had agreed to let the claimant work until the proceeding ends. So, it is concluded that the claimant agreed with the court of appeal decision. However, claimant denied strongly by the fact that the company let him work out of goodwill.

The main argument was that, there were no contract made between the company and the claimant. It was merely out of goodwill. Court of Appeal held that on 1 October 1989, the claimant was justifiable retrenched.

The counsel reiterated that there was never a new employment contract between the claimant and the company. Therefore, there was no unjust dismissal of this case. The underlying issue here is as regards to the "second dismissal" which took effect on 28 February 1999 and the court had to determine whether the dismissal has been without just cause or excuse. The goodwill of the company to allow the claimant to continue working for more than two (2) years pending his leave application is not tantamount to a new contract of employment. The claimant's position was redundant. There was never a new employment contract between the claimant and the company.

By looking at the contents of the letter dated 1 December 1997 and the principle of 'Discharge/Termination Simpliciter" as aforementioned, the court finds that:
1. The claimant was a "temporary" or "casual" employee and he can be terminated without notice by the company.
2. The company in goodwill and compassion agreed to allow the claimant to stay on.

3. In logical explanation, no wise employer will allow its employee to stay on despite the latter's losing a case except that it was done in goodwill and compassion.
4. The company even created a new position for the claimant and the position was redundant.
5. The said letter of termination was justifiably issued.
6. The employment of the claimant is only and until such time as the application of the claimant to the Federal Court is disposed of.
7. Before the said disposal from the Federal Court, the claimant was dismissed by the company.
8. The claimant and his lawyer did nothing for more than two (2) years to have his leave application in the Federal Court heard.
9. The claimant took advantage of the company's goodwill.

Based on the evidence and upon a consideration of the submission of the parties, the court finds that the company had discharged its burden of proof that the claimant was dismissed with just cause or excuse.

Case 5 : Hotel Jaya Puri Bhd v National Union Of Hotel, Bar & Restaurant Workers & Anor

Case No. : 166/76
Award No. : 90 of 1978

The defendant in this case consists of two entities, The Hotel and The Restaurant. Both entities were ordered to be joined as one by the Industrial Court judge as both are legally binding to each other. The issue of this case started when the Restaurant closed its operation entirely and terminated the services of its 56 workers, which were also members of the National Union of Hotel, Bar & Restaurant Workers.

The Union demanded compensations for the retrenched workers by the Restaurant. The court found that the Restaurant was the subsidiary of the Hotel and ordered the Hotel pay the compensation to all the retrenched 56 workers. But the Hotel disregarded the award as the Restaurant is a different entity from the Hotel and therefore appealed to the High Court to quash the award.

The High Court approved the appeal as the termination of service of the workers were proper and legal. It was done due to closure of business as a result of financial losses. The court also stated that there was no law that may interfere with the management's judgement to do so. Hence, the High Court cancelled out the award made by the Industrial Court.

Employers Tips

It is indeed the management's rights in closing its business operations due to various reasons. There is no law that may against a business that decides to close its operations. But, it is best for the management to follow procedures and take precautions to avoid cases like these.

Any retrenchment carried out by organisation must be genuine. The court will always go through all evidence to determine the outcome. Prior to retrenchment, companies should freeze recruitment and transfer staff to similar role as well as to retire those who have reached retirement age.

Employers can refer to The Code of Conduct for Industrial Harmony ("Code") guidelines on best practice for retrenchment exercises. Though it is not legally binding, courts may take into consideration on the employer's practices in determining whether the retrenchment exercise was carried out in a fair manner.

The Code contains suggested criteria for employers to consider when selecting employees for retrenchment. These include, ability, experience, skill and occupation qualifications, age, family situation, length of service, and status (non-citizens, casual, temporary, permanent).

It is likewise a good practice to retrench employees based on the LIFO principle, i.e. "Last In, First Out", where the most junior employee in terms of length of service, in a particular category is selected for retrenchment. It is not mandatory for employers to adhere to this principle, but it is recognised as one of the more objective means of selection.

Employers may depart from the LIFO principle, if they have an alternative, objective selection criteria. LIFO may not be applicable in situations where there is only one employee in the affected category or position.

Having said that, if there are foreign workers in the organisation, the Employment Act 1955 requires that the services of foreign workers be terminated first.

8

CONSTRUCTIVE DISMISSAL

Not all "resignations" are free willed. Constructive dismissal happens when an employee terminates his or her employment due to a breach of contract committed by the employer. The breach of contract is often severe where the essential terms and conditions of the employment contract is altered, leaving the employee no choice but to resign. Though there is no direct dismissal by the employer, it could still amount to unfair dismissal due to the actions of the employer and hence the word "constructive" dismissal.

Grounds for Lawsuit against Employer

Case 1 : Kilang Beras Ban Eng Thye Sdn Bhd v Yacob Bin Noor Mohamed & Anor

Civil Appeal No. : 16-01 of 1995

Yacob and Anor quit without notice and claimed termination benefits and other related claims from the Labour Department under section 19 of the Employment Act 1955 in which employee's salary should be paid not later than the 7th day from the last day of any wage period. The High Court ruled that when the employer fails to pay their employees' salary within the due date, such a breach of contract was, prima facie, wilful and intentional unless satisfactory evidence to the contrary was given by the employer to rebut the inference. The employer explained that the delay was due to quarrels and misunderstandings at its management level. Since the court was not satisfied with this excuse, it upheld the claim of constructive dismissal.

Case 2 : Forari Corp Sdn. Bhd. v. D Sharil Bin Harun

Award No. : 207 of 1988

Industrial Court held the solitary decision of the company to reduce the claimant's salary from RM1,500/- to RM750/- per month, a significant breach and it constitute to constructive dismissal. In this case, it is proven that the employer no longer intends to be bounded by any terms of the contract. Hence, the court finds that the claimant was dismissed constructively.

Case 3 : **Dr. Rayanold Pereira v. Menteri Sumber Manusia & Anor ([1997] 3 CLJ Supp 116)**

A similar case where the employee was not paid and the Industrial tribunal held that this entitled the employee to resign. The resignation was treated as constructive dismissal.

Case 4 : **Kenneison Brothers Sdn Bhd v Selvaratnam**

Award No. : 39 of 1993

The claimant had taken excessive medical leave due to health reasons (psoriasis). It was a genuine case (bona fide) where there was no intention to deceive. However, the company solitarily limited his medical leave to 22 days per year based on the average number of medical leaves taken in the past years, and converted his 'excess medical leave' into no pay leave. The Industrial Court upheld his claim as constructive dismissal stating that by limiting the claimant's medical leave to 22 days after his 14 years of service and converting the excess medical leave into no pay leave, the employer was attempting to vary the essential terms of the claimant's contract of employment.

The Employer Wins

Case 5 : Joo Sim Kee v Patent Licht Bulbs & Lamps Sdn Bhd

Case No. : 9/4-1395/06

Award No. : 819 of 2009

The dispute is about whether Joo Sim Kee ("the claimant") was constructively dismissed or she had abandoned her employment with the company. The claimant was first appointed as a Sales Executive by the company with a monthly salary of RM1,200/- and was later promoted to be a Sales Manager with a monthly salary of RM1,800/-. She was then given a letter of transfer with 24 hours' notice from Penang (head office) to Selangor as her performance was not up to mark. She was supposed to report to a junior in Selangor. Second letter of transfer was issued, but the claimant refused to accept. The Managing Director held her salary by requesting the claimant to collect her salary from the Selangor branch. The claimant also did not answer calls nor return calls to her Managing Director, nor use the new SIM card given by the company. The claimant claimed that she needed time to inform all the customers of the new contact number. A show cause letter was subsequently issued to her for her poor sales performances and failure to answer calls from the bosses and teammates. Apart from that, the claimant had applied for annual leave, but was not approved as she had taken excessive medical leaves and the company deemed that it was reasonable as it is a small company and claimant's performance was poor. She was also found to be quarrelling with her colleagues.

On the other hand, the claimant claimed that she managed to obtain the sales of RM4,045/- in February 2005 within 14 days and RM18,259/- in March 2005 in just two months. She also claimed that she was humiliated and constantly harassed by the Managing Director. Her lunch expenses were not reimbursed when she travelled outstation as the company claimed that such terms do not exist and the claimant did not mention that she was with customers for lunch. When this was brought up to the Managing Director, she was issued a warning letter instead. The claimant had a stressful life working in the organisation as her financial situation was also affected.

Patent Licht Bulbs & Lamps Sdn. Bhd. won this case and the court finds that there was no constructive dismissal as the claimant had abandoned her employment on the 2 August 2005. The court dismissed the claim of the claimant.

Employer's Tips

Constructive Dismissal is where an employer has committed a serious breach of contract, entitling the employee to resign in response to the employer's conduct. The employee is entitled to treat himself or herself as having been "dismissed" and the employer's conduct is often referred to as a "repudiatory breach". This means that, even if the employee were to terminate his or her job, he or she is still entitled to the equivalent amount of remuneration and compensation as been terminated by the employer.

Before the Industrial court applies constructive dismissal, there are a few basic details relating to claims for constructive dismissal:

a. If the dismissal is constructive, the termination of the contract must be as a result of any action, such as stopping work, walking out of his or her employment or resigning from the job on the part of the workman, even though the act may have been the result of pressure from the employer. By virtue of constructive dismissal, industrial law treats some resignations as dismissals and, therefore, extends statutory dismissal rights, mostly payment of compensation and occasionally reinstatement, to those employees who are forced to resign because of their employers' conduct; it does not matter whether the employee left with or without notice, provided he or she was entitled to leave by reason of the employer's conduct.

b. It is for the Industrial Court to decide what constitutes the fundamental term of the contract of employment. The basic starting point is to ask what are the terms which the employer is alleged to have breached. Having identified the terms, the next question is to ask if the said terms were essential terms of the contract of employment. The court will then have to assess the evidence adduced before it to determine whether or not the employer had by his conduct committed such a breach of the contract as to entitle the claimant to consider that he had been constructively dismissed.

c. The Industrial Court in adjudicating the claim of constructive dismissal should confine itself to the issues raised (pleaded) in the employee's statement of claim and those included in the employer's statement in reply. Issues not pleaded are to be discarded by the court; if the Industrial Court considers the issues not pleaded, it is an infringement of the Industrial Court Rules. By considering issues not pleaded by the employee, it is possible for the Industrial Court to uphold the claim of constructive dismissal whereas disregarding those issues not pleaded the court would have arrived at a different decision altogether. Decisions arrived at by the court taking into account issues not pleaded are open to being quashed on the ground that the decisions were tainted as the court is presumed to have taken into account irrelevant considerations.

d. In adjudicating constructive dismissal claims by employees, the Industrial Court would generally have to undertake a two-stage process, that is, after deciding that there was a constructive dismissal, the court should then proceed to determine whether or not the employer had just cause or excuse for bringing about the constructive dismissal. The onus of proving constructive dismissal is on the employee, whereas the burden of proof that the dismissal has been with just cause or excuse lies with the employer.

APPENDIX

CODE OF CONDUCT FOR INDUSTRIAL HARMONY

What is the Code of Conduct for Industrial Harmony?

The Code of Conduct for Industrial Harmony (the Code) is an agreement made between the Ministry of Human Resources (then known as the Ministry of Labour and Manpower) and the Malaysian Council of Employers' Organisations (the predecessor to the Malaysian Employers Federation and the Malaysian Trades Union Congress.

Aim

The aim of the Code is "**to lay down principles and guidelines to employers and workers on the practice of industrial relations for achieving greater industrial harmony**".

Under clause 7 of the Code, the central employer and employee organisations have agreed to endorse and recommend employers and workers to observe and comply with the industrial relations practices agreed upon and accepted by the Ministry of Human Resources.

What the Law States

The Code provides useful guidelines in the area of industrial relations practice. There is no legal obligation on the part of the employer to adhere to the contents of the Code. However, the Code has been given its legal "teeth" by virtue of Sec 30 (5A) of the *Industrial Relations Act 1967*. It states:

"In making its award, the Court may take into consideration any agreement or code relating to employment practices between organisations, representative of employers and workmen respectively where such agreement or code has been approved by the Minister."

Where an employer does not follow the procedures set out in the Code, the employer in fact commits an unfair labour practice. The Industrial Court has been very consistent in its reliance of the Code in retrenchment cases. Failure to follow the Code can result in a retrenchment being declared an unfair dismissal.

Contents of the Code

The Code lists 50 specific industrial relations practices under four broad areas for cooperation, namely:
- Responsibilities
- Employment
- Policy
- Collective Bargaining and Communication
- Consultation.

Responsibilities

At the level of establishment or undertaking
(1) As employers and workers and trade unions representing them are jointly and severally responsible for good industrial relations, the first step is for both management and trade unions to accept, at the highest level, the same degree of responsibility for industrial relations as for other functions within their respective organisations.

Good industrial relations need to be developed within the framework of efficiency of the establishment or undertaking. As such, a major objective of management must be to develop just and effective personnel and industrial relations policies which engender the confidence of all employees, subject to the purpose for which the establishment or undertaking was established and its social obligation to the nation.

Equally, trade unions should ensure that the policies and practices that they adopt are not only fair in relation to the function and purpose for which they have been formed but also take into consideration national interests.

(2) Good industrial relations depend upon good organisation of work. Management should therefore take all reasonable steps to ensure that:

> (a) All management personnel understand their responsibilities and what is required of them, and have the training and authority necessary to discharge such duties and responsibilities efficiently
> (b) Duties and responsibilities for each group of employees are stated with clarity and simplicity in the organisational structure
> (c) Individual employees or work-groups know what their objectives are and are regularly kept informed of progress made towards achieving them

(d) Where possible, work is organised in such manner so that the individual employee has the chance to achieve a sense of job satisfaction.

(3) Where a trade union has been recognised:
    (a) Management should take the initiative in seeking to establish, jointly with the trade union concerned, effective procedures for negotiation, consultation and the settlement of grievances and disputes
    (b) Management and the trade union should take all reasonable steps to ensure that both the management and union personnel observe agreements reached and use agreed procedures
    (c) Management should not discourage employees from joining the recognised union and from taking an active part in its legitimate activities.

(4) The supervisor is management's first "contact" man with the employees and special attention should be given to his appointment and his needs on the job. The employer should ensure that he:
    (a) is technically proficient and adequately trained and possesses the personal qualities required to exercise supervision
    (b) Has charge of a work-group of a size that he can supervise effectively
    (c) Is an effective link in the interchange of information and views between senior management and members of his work group
    (d) Is briefed about innovations and changes before they occur so that he can explain management's policies and intentions to his work-group.

At national or industry level

(5) Employers' association should:

(a) Co-operate with the trade unions in establishing effective procedures at industry or national level for the negotiation of terms and conditions of employment and for the settlement of disputes

(b) Encourage the establishment of effective procedures among member organisations for the settlement of grievances and disputes at the level of the establishment or undertaking

(c) Take all reasonable steps to ensure that member organisations observe agreements and agreed procedures

(d) Collect, analyse and distribute information to its members concerning industrial relations matters

(e) Identify trends and new developments in industrial relations and help its members to anticipate and keep abreast of change

(f) Provide an efficient and realistic advisory service to its members on all matters of industrial relations.

(6) A trade union can promote the interests of its members effectively only if it accepts, that, in common with management, it has an interest in and a responsibility for the success of the undertaking and for the national, economic and social well-being of the country as a whole. This involves co-operation with the employer in promoting efficiency and good industrial relations.

(7) To secure these aims, a trade union should:

    (a) Co-operate with employers' association in establishing effective procedures at industry level for the negotiation of terms and conditions of employment and for the settlement of disputes that arise

    (b) Co-operate with individual management in establishing effective procedures for negotiation, consultation, communication and the settlement of grievances and disputes

> (c) Take all reasonable steps to ensure that their officials and members observe agreements and use agreed procedures
>
> (d) Make full use of the established procedures for the settlement of disputes.

(8) To ensure that its organisation is effective, a trade union should also:

> (a) Have enough officials, full time or otherwise, to maintain regular contacts not only with union members but also with management of establishments or undertakings where the union has been recognised
>
> (b) Maintain a communications system which secures the interchange of information and views between different levels in the union and ensures that members are systematically and regularly kept informed, factually and objectively, of the progress of negotiations for a collective agreement
>
> (c) Encourage its members to attend union meetings and to participate fully in union activities by holding branch meetings at times and at places convenient to the majority; and, where there is a large enough membership, consider forming the branch organisation of the establishment
>
> (d) Establish effective procedures for the settlement of disputes among members of the union.

(9) The trade union should also ensure that all its officials:

> (a) Clearly know and understand the nature and extent of their responsibilities and authority
>
> (b) Are adequately trained to look after members' interests in a responsible and efficient way
>
> (c) Wherever possible and practicable, hold regular dialogues with officials of employers' association and its members.

(10) As the basic relationship between an employer and the individual employee is defined in the individual contract of employment, it should be expressed in clear and precise language. It is the employee's responsibility to satisfy himself that he or she understands the terms of the contract and to abide by them.

(11) The employer and relevant trade union should ensure that procedures for dealing with questions that arise on the individual contract of employment are clearly laid down. But it is the responsibility of the employer himself to:
> (a) Familiarise himself with these procedures and
> (b) Make use of them when the need arises.

Employment policy

(12) A sound employment policy is a prerequisite to good employer-employee relations. It should also reflect the Government's policy requirements, announced from time to time. Good planning and efficient use of manpower are important both for the success of the establishment and for the security of those employed in it. The employer should, therefore:
> (a) Keep fluctuations in manpower requirements to a minimum by means of advance planning
> (b) Make changes, wherever necessary, with as little disruption as is necessary
> (c) Where practicable, maintain, in consultation with the employees or their representatives or trade union, as appropriate, a scheme for transferring employees from one job to another within the establishment or undertaking so that unavoidable changes in manpower requirements can be handled smoothly.

Recruitment

(13) Recruitment and selection policy can help good industrial relations by ensuring that workers are engaged for jobs suited to their abilities. The employer should, therefore:
> (a) Define the qualifications and experience needed for the vacant job
> (b) Ensure that selection is based on suitability for the job
> (c) Consider filling the vacancy by transfer or promotion before trying to recruit from outside
> (d) Explain the terms and conditions of employment to applicants before they are engaged
> (e) Ensure that those who carry out recruitment and selection are competent to do so and that the recruitment and selection methods are regularly checked to be effective.

Training

(14) Adequately trained employees are essential for the success of the undertaking. Training appropriate to his work also helps the individual to develop his potential, to increase the satisfaction he finds in his work and to improve his earning capacity.

(15) Newly recruited employees should be given initial instruction covering:
> (a) The organisation, its employment policy and welfare and social facilities that are available
> (b) Specific training in the job to supplement previous training and experience.

(16) Younger persons entering employment or the first time should be given broader basic instructions covering a general introduction to working life.

(17) In appropriate cases, further training should be provided when there is a significant change in the content of the job or in the level of the job being performed.

Payment system

(18) Although payment systems vary according to the nature and organisation of the work, local conditions and other factors, the following principles should be observed so as to ensure that the system of payment is soundly based and thereby reduces the incidence of disputes arising:

> (a) Payment systems should be as simple as possible
> (b) Differences in rates should be related to the requirements of the job which should, wherever possible, be assessed by agreed as well established methods
> (c) Piece-work rates, incentive bonuses, etc should be determined by agreed or well established methods
> (d) Rates of payment should be jointly negotiated where a recognised trade union exists.

Security of employment

(19) Insecurity of employment and fear of the consequences of redundancy and retirement have a major influence on attitudes to work and good industrial relations. Consistent with the efficiency and success of the undertaking, the employer should provide greatest possible stability in terms of job tenure. The employer should also, where practicable:

> (a) Offer prospects for advancement and promotion within the undertaking with opportunities for any necessary training
> (b) Provide retirement, retrenchment and sick pay schemes to supplement statutory provisions.

Redundancy and retrenchment

(20) In circumstances where redundancy is likely an employer should, in consultation with his employees' representatives or their trade union, as appropriate, and in consultation with the Ministry of Labour and Manpower, take positive steps to avert or minimise reductions of workforce by the adoption of appropriate measures such as:

    (a) Limitation on recruitment
    (b) Restriction of overtime work
    (c) Restriction of work on weekly day of rest
    (d) Reduction in number of shifts or days worked a week
    (e) Reduction in the number of hours of work
    (f) Re-training and/or transfer to other department/work.

(21) The ultimate responsibility for deciding on the size of the workforce must rest with the employer, but before any decision on reduction is taken, there should be consultation with the workers or their trade union representatives on the reduction.

(22) (a) If retrenchment becomes necessary, despite having taken appropriate measures, the employer should take the following measures:

    (i) Giving as early a warning, as practicable, to the workers concerned

    (ii) Introducing schemes for voluntary retrenchment and retirement and for payment of redundancy and retirement benefits

    (iii) Retiring workers who are beyond their normal retiring age

    (iv) Assisting, in co-operation with the Ministry of Human Resources, the workers to find work outside the undertaking

(v) Spreading termination of employment over a longer period

(vi) Ensuring that no such announcement is made before the workers and their representatives or trade union has been informed.

(b) The employer should select employees to be retrenched in accordance with objective criteria. Such criteria, which should have been worked out in advance with the employees' representatives or trade union may include:

(i) The need for the efficient operation of the establishment or undertaking

(ii) Ability, experience, skill and occupational qualifications of individual workers required by the establishment or undertaking under part (i)

(iii) Consideration for length of service and status (non-citizens, casual, temporary, permanent)

(iv) Age

(v) Family situation

(vi) Such other criteria as may be formulated in the context of national policies.

(23) Employees, who are retrenched, should be given priority of engagement/re-engagement, as far as is possible, by the employer when he engages workers.

(24) The appropriate measures and objective criteria should comprise part of the establishments or undertaking's employment policy.

Working conditions

(25) Good physical working conditions help to achieve good industrial relations. The first need is for the employer to ensure that the standards laid down by law are fully complied with.

But this is not enough by itself, for most work-places could be made safe, healthier and more pleasant to work in if more care were taken about the working environment — like improving the cleanliness, tidiness and general appearance of the work-place; reducing strain and monotony involved in the work; encouraging workers and their representatives to co-operate in improving working conditions and providing for consultation with workers on their representatives on these matters. Workers or their trade union representatives should co-operate with employers in making the best use of the arrangements for consultation in this field.

www.ingramcontent.com/pod-product-compliance
Lightning Source LLC
Chambersburg PA
CBHW030846180526
45163CB00004B/1466